ELECTRICITY
Experiments
for Children

ELECTRICITY
Experiments
for Children

Formerly titled ELECTRONICS FOR CHILDREN

by Gabriel Reuben

Illustrated by Bernard Case

Dover Publications, Inc., New York

Published in Canada by General Publishing Company, Ltd.,
30 Lesmill Road, Don Mills, Toronto, Ontario.

Published in the United Kingdom by Constable and Company, Ltd.,
10 Orange Street, London WC 2.

This Dover edition, first published in 1968, is an unabridged
and unaltered republication of the work originally published in
1960 under the title *Electronics for Children*. The work is re-
printed by special arrangement with Sterling Publishing Co., Inc.,
publisher of the original edition.

International Standard Book Number: 0-486-22030-3
Library of Congress Catalog Card Number: 68-9307

Manufactured in the United States of America

Dover Publications, Inc.
180 Varick Street
New York, N. Y. 10014

CONTENTS

BEFORE YOU BEGIN

Learning by doing is the quickest and surest way to understanding. Instead of just reading about how and why something works, you perform experiments yourself and actually see what happens. The experiments in this book will help you to understand magnetism, electricity, electronics and nuclear energy — all subjects that are becoming more and more important in today's world.

With simple equipment, most of which you already have at home, you can set up your own laboratory in a corner of a room and follow in the footsteps of the great scientists, many of whom began their lifelong interest when they were young.

It is a good idea to perform the experiments in the order in which they are given, because each one depends, to a large extent, on the knowledge gained in those that came before. Before beginning any experiment, read all the directions carefully. You'll be anxious to begin immediately, of course, but two of the foremost requirements of a scientist are patience and discipline. After you understand what you are to do, assemble all the equipment you will need. Then, read each step through again before performing it. Refer to the illustrations to make sure you've set the equipment up correctly, and, most important, *think* about what you are doing and why. Some of the experiments may look complicated at first, but you will find, as you go methodically from step to step, that everything fits into place. If, by chance, you don't succeed the first time, try to figure out what went wrong, and begin again. Another essential trait of a scientist is perseverance, or what some people call "stick-to-itiveness."

While all of the experiments in this book are safe, you must exercise ordinary care and use your common sense. If you follow the directions, everything will work out well. Where warnings are given, be sure to heed them.

After you finish each experiment, store your equipment neatly. Then, if you want to do the experiment again some other time, or go on to the next one, you will find everything easily.

You will soon discover that learning by doing is fun. You will also get great satisfaction from understanding more deeply some of the forces in nature that you see and use every day of your life.

MAGNETISM

Magnetism is the power of certain stones and metals to attract each other. According to legend, the discovery of magnetism occurred about 3000 years ago in an ancient Middle Eastern country called Magnesia.

One day, the story goes, a shepherd found it difficult to lift his iron-tipped staff from certain places on the ground. After investigating, he realized that he had difficulty only when the iron tip was on a certain type of dark stone. These stones were *loadstones* (sometimes spelled "lodestone"), which contain a kind of iron ore called *magnetite*.

Since magnetism became known, man has found out much about this power and devised many uses for it. With the aid of science, he has also learned to impart magnetism to certain metals which do not possess it naturally.

WHAT WILL A MAGNET ATTRACT?

Gather the following equipment: A magnet and samples of as many different substances as you are able to find — wood, metals, liquids, rubber, cloth, and so forth. Try to get samples of as many *elements* as you can locate. Elements are the basic substance of which all matter is made — all liquids, all solids, all gases — even air, which is a mixture of gases. An element is made up of only one kind of atom. Scientists have found 92 elements in nature and have created 10 artificial elements. It is quite possible that in the future they will be able to make more artificial elements. For your experiment, you can probably find objects made of iron, copper, gold, or silver, which are all natural elements. On page 81 there is a list of all the known elements.

Follow this procedure: Touch the magnet to each of the materials you have gathered, and then slowly pull it away.

You will observe: The magnet attracts only those objects which contain iron, nickel or cobalt.

Although you can only see the effects of magnetism on iron, nickel and cobalt, scientists believe that magnetism has some effect on all substances. For all practical purposes, however, we say that it affects only iron, nickel and cobalt.

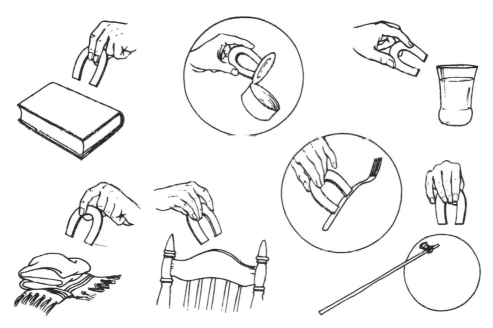

WILL MAGNETISM PASS THROUGH MATERIALS?

Gather the following equipment: A magnet; several paper clips, or any other small objects which you know will be affected by magnetism; a piece of string; some cellophane tape; a drinking glass; a small piece of plywood; a dishpan filled to a depth of about 3 inches with water; a book; and an empty can.

Follow this procedure: 1. Place the clips in the glass. Then place the magnet beneath the glass as close to the clips as possible. Move the magnet slowly along the surface of the glass.

You will observe: The clips inside the glass follow the movements of the magnet outside the glass.

2. Tie one of the clips to the string. Fasten the other end of the string to a table. Lift the clip until the string is taut; then hold the magnet about ¼ of an inch from the clip and let go of the clip. Move the magnet slowly to the left and right, keeping it the same distance from the clip. Then gradually increase the distance between the clip and the magnet.

You will observe: The clip is attracted by the magnet and holds the string taut as long as the magnet is close to the clip. When you move the magnet more than ½ an inch away from the clip, the string falls.

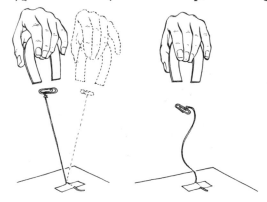

3. Place the clips on the piece of plywood. Then hold the magnet on the underside of the plywood, directly under the clips. Move the magnet slowly along the plywood.

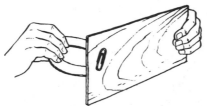

You will observe: The clips are attracted by the magnet and move along the plywood as you move the magnet on the other side.

4. Place the clips in the dishpan of water. Then put the magnet in the water and move it very close, within a range of 1/4 of an inch from the clips.

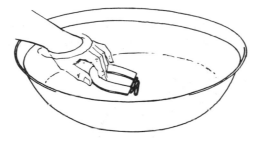

You will observe: The magnet attracts the clips in the water.

5. Place the clips on the front cover of the book. Hold the magnet against the back cover of the book and move it slowly.

You will observe: The clips do not follow the movements of the magnet.

6. Open the cover and three pages of the book. Place some clips on the inside of the open cover and between each of the three pages. Hold the

magnet on the outside of the open cover, just opposite the clips, and move the magnet slowly.

You will observe: The clips are attracted by the magnet and follow its movements along the other side of the cover.

7. Put the clips in the can. Move the magnet along the bottom and sides of the can.

You will observe: The clips are attracted by the magnet and move along the inside of the can as you move the magnet along the outside of it.

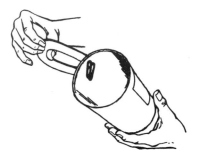

Magnetism will pass through any material, as long as the distance or thickness is not too great. The stronger the magnet is, the greater will be the distance of its power of attraction.

CAN YOU FEEL MAGNETISM?

Gather the following equipment: A magnet and a nail.

Follow this procedure: 1. Hold the magnet with one hand and move it over the palm and back of your other hand, keeping it about ½ an inch away from the flesh. Now move the magnet close to your lips, your cheeks, and your wrists.

You will observe: The magnet causes no feeling.

2. Hold the magnet in one hand and the nail in the other. Bring the two about ½ an inch from each other. Allow the magnet and nail to touch. Pull them apart.

You will observe: When you bring the magnet close enough, it attracts the nail and you must exert force to pull it away.

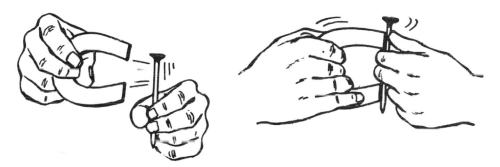

You cannot feel magnetism itself, but you can feel the force it exerts.

CAN YOU SEE MAGNETISM?

Gather the following equipment: A magnet; a sheet of paper; and some iron filings.

Follow this procedure: 1. Place some of the iron filings on the sheet of paper. Move the magnet close enough to the filings to attract them. Watch carefully as the filings jump to the magnet.

You will observe: You cannot see the force of magnetism attracting the filings.

2. Place the magnet under the sheet of paper. Shake the iron filings on the paper just over the magnet and around it.

You will observe: The filings on the paper form a pattern around the *poles* (ends) of the magnet.

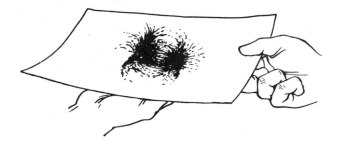

You cannot see magnetism itself, but you can see what magnetism does. With the aid of iron filings, you can see the area around a magnet in which it exerts its force. This area is called the magnet's *field of force* or *magnetic field*. The lines formed by the filings are called *lines of force*.

HOW DO THE POLES OF A MAGNET ACT?

Gather the following equipment: Two bar magnets; a piece of string; a shaker of iron filings; and a sheet of paper.

Follow this procedure: 1. Tie the string around the center of one of the magnets so that the magnet balances like a see-saw when you hold it from the string. When you hold a magnet so that it can turn freely — on the end of a string, for example — one end automatically points toward the south. This end is called the south-seeking or *south pole* of the magnet. The other end automatically points toward the north, and is called the north-seeking or *north pole* of the magnet. The ends are often marked "N" for North and "S" for South. Bring the south pole of the untied magnet close to the south pole of the magnet on the string.

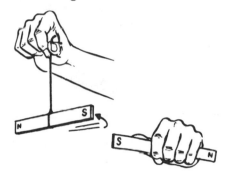

You will observe: The south pole of the tied magnet repels the south pole of the other magnet.

2. Bring the north pole of the free magnet close to the north pole of the tied magnet.

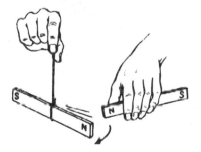

You will observe: The north pole of the tied magnet repels the north pole of the other magnet.

3. Bring the north pole of the free magnet close to the south pole of the magnet on the string.

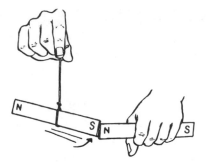

You will observe: The north pole of one magnet attracts the south pole of the other.

4. Place both bar magnets on a flat surface with the north pole of one magnet about ½ inch away from the north pole of the other. Place a sheet of paper over the magnets. Shake some iron filings over the covered magnets.

You will observe: The lines of force traced by the iron filings show that the two poles are repelling each other.

5. Repeat the same procedure, but put the south poles close to each other.

You will observe: The lines of force traced by the iron filings again show that the two like poles are repelling each other.

6. Repeat the same procedure, but this time put the north pole of one magnet close to the south pole of the other.

You will observe: The lines of force traced by the iron filings show that the two poles are attracting each other.

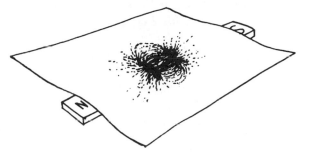

Like poles repel each other. Unlike poles attract each other. Both the north and south poles of magnets attract nickel, iron and cobalt.

HOW CAN YOU MAKE A TEMPORARY MAGNET?

Gather the following equipment: A magnet; a nail; a few straight pins; an iron bolt; and a hammer.

Follow this procedure: 1. Hold the magnet in one hand. With your other hand, rub the nail lengthwise along one of the poles of the magnet. Be sure to rub in only one direction, either upward or downward. After two minutes of rubbing, try to pick up one or more of the pins with the point of the nail.

You will observe: The nail becomes a temporary magnet and picks up a few of the pins.

2. Hold the iron bolt in one hand. Stand facing north, and point the bolt downward at about a 25-degree angle. Then, with a hammer, gently tap that end of the bolt which is nearer to you. Tap for about a minute. Next, try to pick up some of the pins with that end of the bolt which is farther from you.

You will observe: The bolt becomes a temporary magnet and picks up a few of the pins.

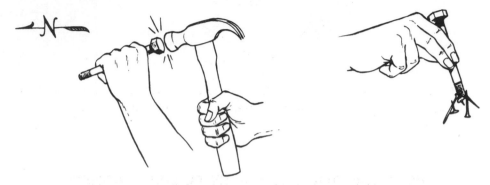

Iron is the softest of the three metals which are affected by magnetism. It is the easiest one to make into a magnet, but it loses its magnetism rapidly. A *temporary magnet,* made as in this experiment, retains its magnetic power for only a few days. See page 24 for an explanation of why this is so.

HOW CAN YOU MAKE AN ELECTROMAGNET?

Gather the following equipment: A 1½-volt dry cell; a pencil; a nail; several paper clips; and about 4 feet of very thin, insulated copper wire.

Follow this procedure: 1. Scrape off or pull back about ½ inch of the insulation from both ends of the wire. Do the same thing with a section near the middle of the wire. Connect one end of the wire to one of the terminals of the dry cell and the other end of the wire to the other terminal. Try to pick up some of the clips with the middle section of the wire where you scraped off the insulation. Disconnect the wire from one of the terminals.

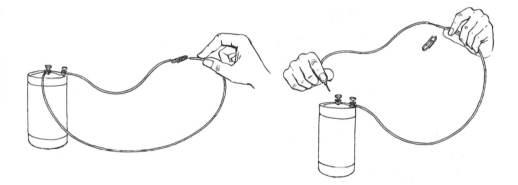

You will observe: The wire picks up one or two of the clips, but they drop when you disconnect the wire from one of the terminals.

2. Coil the wire around the pencil, but leave enough wire at each end to connect to the terminals. Remove the pencil and scrape off a little of the insulation at only one end of the coil, just before the point where it becomes straight. Connect each straight end of the wire to one of the terminals. Try to pick up some of the clips with the scraped end of the coil.

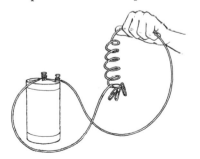

You will observe: The coiled wire holds three or four clips.

3. Coil another wire tightly around the nail. Connect the ends of the wire to the dry cell, as you did in the first two parts of this experiment. Holding one end of the nail, try to pick up some of the clips with the other end of it. Disconnect the wire from one of the terminals when you have finished.

You will observe: The nail picks up five or six of the clips.

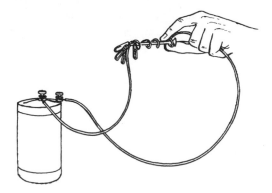

An electric current flowing through a wire makes the wire magnetic. When you coil the wire, its magnetic power is stronger, and when you put a soft iron core inside the coil, the magnetic power is even stronger. *Electromagnets* — objects in which magnetism is induced by electricity — are temporary magnets. When the current is off, the electromagnet loses its power.

HOW CAN YOU MAKE A PERMANENT MAGNET?

Gather the following equipment: About 4 feet of very thin, insulated copper wire; a pencil; two 1½-volt dry cells; several paper clips; and a screw driver.

Follow this procedure: Snip off a piece of wire 4 inches long. Scrape the ends of the wire clean of insulation so that the copper is exposed. With the wire, connect the *negative terminal* (the one on the edge) of one dry cell with the *positive terminal* (the one in the middle) of the other dry cell. Be sure the copper makes contact with the terminals. Now take the other piece of wire. Leave 9 inches of it straight at each end; coil the remainder of it around the whole length of the pencil. Then remove the pencil. Place a metal portion of the screw driver in the coil. Scrape the ends of the wire free of insulation. Connect one end of the wire to the free terminal on one of the dry cells. Connect the other end of the wire to the free terminal on the other dry cell. After about 15 seconds, disconnect one of the wires from its terminal connection. Remove the screw driver from the coil and try to pick up some of the clips with the screw driver.

You will observe: The screw driver picks up several clips.

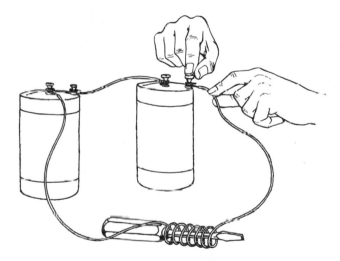

You have just made what is called a *permanent magnet,* but like all so-called permanent magnets, its magnetic power will last only a few years, not forever. If the metal were iron, it would lose its magnetic power quickly. Screw drivers, however, like most metal tools, are not made of pure iron, but rather of steel, which is an iron *alloy*. An alloy is a combination of metals, or metals and other substances, melted together to form a new compound. Steel is an alloy of iron and carbon. Alloys with magnetic metals make stronger magnets and hold their magnetism for longer periods of time.

HOW CAN YOU MAKE A COMPASS?

Gather the following equipment: A bar magnet; a 6-inch piece of thread; a needle; a pin; a small piece of cellophane tape; an empty jar with a cover; and a compass.

Follow this procedure: 1. Tie one end of the thread around the middle of the magnet so that the magnet balances when you hold it by the thread. When the magnet stops swaying, see which way the north pole is pointing. Compare this with the way the compass needle is pointing.

WARNING: Don't let the magnet get too close to the compass. The magnet can attract the compass needle and weaken its effectiveness.

You will observe: When the magnet comes to rest, the north pole points north.

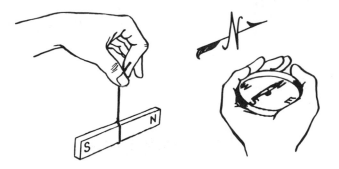

2. Rub the needle lengthwise along one of the poles of the magnet; each stroke must be in the same direction, not back and forth. When the needle is magnetized enough to attract the pin, tie the thread around the middle of the needle so that it balances. Tape the other end of the thread

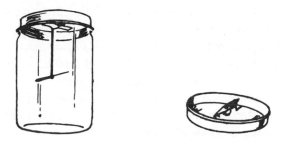

to the inside of the jar cover. Lower the needle into the jar so that it hangs freely when you tighten the cover. Compare the way the compass and the needle point.

You will observe: The needle is now a compass. It points north, as does the compass.

The earth itself is a tremendous magnet. The magnetic poles of the earth are said to be huge deposits of magnetite. The north magnetic pole is about 1400 miles away from the geographic North Pole, and the south magnetic pole is about 1400 miles away from the geographic South Pole. The earth's magnetic poles change position from time to time. Magnets are attracted to the magnetic poles. This is why the poles of magnets are called north-seeking and south-seeking, and why magnets can serve as compasses.

Because the magnetic poles and geographic poles are not at the same place, mariners and others who must get accurate information from their compasses correct their compass reading with a chart which compensates for the error of the compass in various locations. The disparity between the magnetic and geographic poles is called the *angle of declination*. The magnet points to true north only in those places which lie in a straight line with the north geographic pole and the north magnetic pole.

It is said that the earth's magnetic field causes objects made of iron, nickel or cobalt anywhere in the world to become magnetized if they remain unmoved for very long periods of time.

HOW CAN YOU TELL TIME WITH A COMPASS?

Gather the following equipment: A compass and a pencil.

Follow this procedure: Take the equipment outdoors on a sunny day. Stand facing north. Hold the pencil in line with the compass needle, but at an upward angle of 45 degrees; the bottom end of the pencil should rest on the glass directly above the "S" on the face of the compass.

You will observe: The pencil casts a shadow over the compass. If you regard the "N" on the compass as 12 o'clock, the "W" as 9 o'clock, the "E" as 3 o'clock, and the "S" as 6 o'clock, the shadow gives you the approximate time.

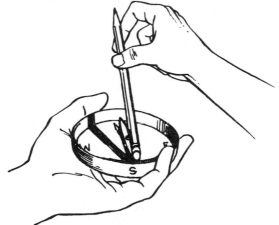

Of course, you must have sunlight for this experiment to work. The hour you get will be in terms of standard time. You will recognize that, as a means of telling time, the compass operates in much the same fashion as a sundial.

WHAT HAPPENS WHEN YOU CUT A MAGNET INTO PIECES?

Gather the following equipment: A hack saw and an inexpensive bar magnet.

Follow this procedure: 1. Saw the magnet into thirds. Put the magnet together again as it was by placing the pieces side by side.

You will observe: The parts of the magnet attract each other when you replace them exactly as they were before you sawed them apart.

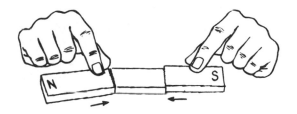

2. Pull the two ends away from the middle. Turn them around so that what were the north and south poles of the unsawed magnet are now pointing inward toward the center piece. Move them toward the center piece.

You will observe: The center piece repels each end piece.

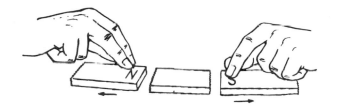

3. Take each of the three pieces of the magnet in turn and place first one end and then the other about 1/4 of an inch from the hack-saw blade.

You will observe: In each case the hack-saw blade is attracted to the magnet.

When you cut or break a magnet, the cut or broken end becomes the opposite pole to the one on the other end.

A broken magnet does retain its magnetic power, but striking, dropping or vibrating a magnet, as you did when you sawed it apart, weakens it considerably. Magnets also become weaker when they are heated. Bear this in mind, and remember to handle and store magnets with care.

WHAT IS THE SECRET OF MAGNETISM?

Scientists have not been able to prove what causes magnetism, but most of them accept an explanation called the *molecule theory*. This theory is based on the fact that all matter is made up of *molecules,* small groupings of *atoms,* which are in turn the smallest particles into which elements can be divided and still be recognizable. The molecules of iron, nickel and cobalt, according to this theory, are themselves little magnets, each with a north-seeking and a south-seeking pole. The theory goes on to explain that when the "molecule-magnets" of these metals are arranged at random, with the poles pointing in all directions, these metals do not behave like magnets. When the molecules of these metals are pulled into line with all the north-seeking poles pointing in one direction, and all the south-seeking poles pointing in the opposite direction, then these metals behave like magnets.

In temporary magnets, made of "soft" (pure) iron, the molecules soon become disarranged again. Permanent magnets, made of "hard" alloys, hold the "molecule-magnets" in line for years.

This theory also explains why cobalt, nickel and iron objects become magnetized after lying unmoved for years; their "molecule-magnets," subject to the earth's magnetic field for so long, are gradually pulled into line. Similarly, you can make a magnet by tapping an iron bolt while pointing it in the direction of the north magnetic pole, because the tapping and the influence of the earth's magnetic pole combine to jar the "molecule-magnets" of the bolt into line.

According to this theory, the explanation of why magnets weaken when they are dropped or struck is that the blow jars the "molecule-magnets" out of line. In the same way, when you heat magnets, the heat sets the "molecule-magnets" into motion, disorganizes them, and thus makes the magnet grow weaker.

Another theory scientists put forth to explain magnetism is the *electron theory*. This theory holds that the *electrons* of iron, nickel and cobalt cause magnetism. Electrons are unbelievably tiny particles of the atom that circulate around its core, or *nucleus*. The people who support this theory point out that electrons circulate around the nucleus of the atom in a variety of directions. The supporters of this theory say that when the electrons of iron, nickel or cobalt are caused to circulate in the same direction, by an electric current, for example, they set up in these metals a current, which is magnetism. This theory is less widely accepted than the molecule theory.

HOW CAN YOU MAKE AN ELECTRIC CURRENT WITH A MAGNET?

Gather the following equipment: About 4 feet of copper bell wire; a compass; and a bar magnet.

Follow this procedure: Scrape the insulation from both ends of the wire. Leaving about a foot of wire straight at each end, coil the remainder around four of your fingers. Remove your fingers from inside the completed coil. Splice the ends of the wire so that the exposed copper at each end makes contact with that at the other end. Holding the compass under one of the straight ends of wire, move one of the poles of the magnet in and out of the coil.

You will observe: The needle on the compass jiggles back and forth as you move the magnet in and out of the coil. This shows that an electric current is flowing through the wire.

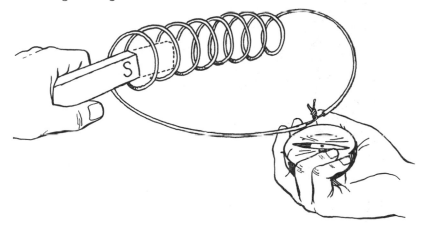

Placing a wire across a moving magnetic field causes a current to flow through the wire. An electric current must have an unbroken path through a conductor. Such a path is called a *circuit*.

Now that you have actually made an electric current by means of magnetism, it is time to delve into the subject of electricity and to perform experiments that will enable you to observe its effects. You have already gained some notion of the close relationship between magnetism and electricity — the ability of magnetism to induce electricity and vice versa. You will soon discover that these two phenomena generally occur in such close association with one another that it is almost impossible in actual practice to deal with them separately.

ELECTRICITY

Electricity is the movement of many electrons (see page **76**) in a particular direction from one atom to another.

The first mention of electrical phenomena in history tells us that about 2500 years ago the Greeks found they could make amber attract certain objects by rubbing it with a goatskin. People attempted little more with this "magic" until the year 1600, when William Gilbert, an English scientist, performed experiments to learn more about it. He is generally credited with originating the term "electric," probably taking it from *"elektron,"* the Greek word for amber. Just a little more than 100 years ago, the Englishman Michael Faraday and other scientists began to learn enough about electricity to explore ways of using it.

HOW CAN YOU GET ELECTRICITY BY RUBBING?

Gather the following equipment: A glass rod; a piece of silk; about 10 inches of thread; a pair of scissors; a piece of soft wool; a piece of hard rubber (from an old tire) ; a pair of leather-soled shoes; and a door mat or rug.

Follow this procedure: 1. Cut the thread into about a dozen pieces. Rub the glass rod vigorously for a few moments with the piece of silk. Then move the glass rod very close to the pieces of thread.

You will observe: The glass rod attracts the threads.

The kind of electricity you have just created is called *static electricity,* because it does not flow in a current. The silk cloth rubs some of the electrons from the surface of the glass rod, creating on the rod an imbalance called a *positive* charge. A substance whose atoms are lacking in electrons has a positive charge. When you bring the glass rod close to the threads, the rod "pulls" at the electrons on them.

2. Rub the piece of rubber vigorously with the soft wool. Then move the rubber close to the threads.

You will observe: The rubber attracts the threads.

This is also static electricity but in this case, the charge is *negative.* The rubber took electrons from the piece of wool. Substances whose atoms have an excess of electrons are negatively charged.

3. Wearing the leather-soled shoes, scuff your feet on the door mat for about 15 seconds; don't touch any surface with your hands until you have finished scuffing. Then touch a metal door knob.

You will observe: A charge of static electricity momentarily "tickles" the part of your hand which first touches the knob. The friction between your feet and the door mat built up a charge in your body. If it is a particularly cold and dry day, you may see a spark and hear it "pop" as it jumps from your hand to the knob. You may have difficulty in getting this experiment to work satisfactorily during the summer or on a damp day.

Damp or moist air is a good *conductor* of electricity, which means that electrons move through it easily. As a result, it carries electrons away, making it difficult to accumulate enough of them for a charge. Similarly, metals, which are also good conductors of electricity, will not build static electrical charges. Materials that do not conduct electricity are called non-conductors or *insulators*. It is with insulators that you can build static charges.

HOW CAN YOU DETERMINE WHAT MATERIALS ARE CONDUCTORS?

Gather the following equipment: A 1½-volt dry cell; two 8-inch lengths of copper wire; a demonstration flashlight socket (a special kind of socket for experiments) ; a flashlight bulb; and pieces of different materials, including rock, cloth, wood, metals, glass and so forth.

Follow this procedure: Scrape the insulation from the ends of both pieces of wire. Connect the wires from one of the terminals on the dry cell to one of the connections on the demonstration socket. Screw the bulb into the socket until it lights. Disconnect the wire from one of the terminals. Then, one by one, place the materials you have gathered between the terminal and the wire you have just disconnected so that the material touches both the terminal of the dry cell and the end of the wire.

You will observe: The bulb lights up whenever the material you use to complete the circuit is a conductor. It does not light when the material you use is a non-conductor.

For an explanation of why some materials are good conductors while others are not, see page 69.

HOW CAN YOU MAKE AN ELECTROSCOPE?
(An Instrument for Detecting Electric Charges)

Gather the following equipment: A jar or bottle with a cork or rubber stopper to fit it; a paper clip or a 6-inch piece of copper wire; a strip of aluminum foil about 3 inches long and 1 inch wide; a comb; a test tube; a piece of silk and a piece of wool.

Follow this procedure: Straighten the clip. Push one end of the clip through the center of the stopper so that only about ½ inch of it sticks up through the top and some of it goes through the bottom. Make a little hook or "L" at the bottom end of the clip. Fold the aluminum foil in half so that each half is 1½ inches long. Cut a piece of the foil off at the fold so that the two halves are held together by only a very narrow strip. Hang the foil on the "L" at the bottom of the clip. Lower the clip and foil into the jar and seal the jar with the stopper. Rub the comb vigorously with the wool and then touch the comb to the bit of metal sticking through the stopper. Rub it back and forth on the metal for a moment. Now touch the piece of metal sticking

up through the stopper with your finger. Follow this by rubbing the test tube with the silk and then touching the metal sticking up through the stopper with the test tube. Rub it back and forth for a moment.

You will observe: When you touch the metal with the comb, the folded aluminum foil moves apart. When you touch the metal with your finger, the two halves of the foil come together. When you touch the metal with the test tube, the halves of the aluminum foil move apart again.

The jar with the stopper, clip and aluminum foil is a simple type of electroscope — an instrument designed to reveal the presence of an electrical charge on an object. When a charged object touches the metal, the metal acts as a conductor and carries the charge to the aluminum foil. Since it carries the same charge to both halves of the foil, the halves repel each other and fly apart. Either a positive or negative charge produces the same reaction. When a hand touches the metal, the charge leaks off. If an uncharged object touched the metal before a charged object, the foil would be unaffected.

HOW CAN YOU MAKE AN ELECTROPHORUS?
(An Instrument for Building Static Electric Charges)

Gather the following equipment: A phonograph record; a piece of wool, fur or soft leather; a metal jar cover; a stick of wood 6 inches long and 1 inch wide or some other insulator of the same dimensions; and a nail.

Follow this procedure: Balance the inside of the cover on the stick. Nail it to the stick in that position. Rub the phonograph record vigorously with the wool for about 15 seconds. Hold the cover by the stick-handle and place it on the part of the phonograph record which you just rubbed. For only a second, touch a finger of your free hand to the metal cover and to the phonograph record at the same time. Take the cover away from the record by the handle. Move your free hand very close to the edge of the cover.

You will observe: A spark jumps from the cover to your hand.

On a particularly cold and dry day, you can get several sparks in succession from an electrophorus like this without recharging the record (rubbing it again) . Just place the metal cover on the record and touch both at the same time with your finger. Incidentally, use a record you no longer want, because it will be scratched during the experiment.

HOW CAN YOU MAKE A BATTERY?

Gather the following equipment: A strip of zinc, 1 inch wide and 6½ inches long; a strip of copper of the same size; a small piece of steel wool or sandpaper; a demonstration flashlight socket; a flashlight bulb; 12 inches of bell wire; a large piece of blotting paper or cotton; some ammonium chloride — available in well-equipped drug stores and chemical supply houses (heavily salted water will do but not as well) ; an eye dropper; and a rubber band.

Follow this procedure: Cut the copper and zinc each into five pieces 1 inch in length and one piece 1½ inches in length. Punch a tiny hole at one end of each of the 1½-inch-long pieces of metal. Cut the bell wire into two 6-inch lengths. Scrape the insulation back from all four ends. Connect an end of one of the pieces of wire to the piece of zinc with the hole in it, putting the wire through the hole. In the same manner, connect an end of the other piece of wire to the piece of copper with the hole in it. Rub all of the pieces of metal with the steel wool. Cut the blotting paper into eleven 1-inch squares. Place a square of blotting paper on the piece of zinc that has the wire attached. Fill the eye dropper with ammonium chloride and soak the blotting paper on the zinc with it. Then, alternately pile copper, saturated blotting paper, zinc, blotting paper, copper, and so forth until you have the

piece of copper with the wire attached on top. Remember to soak each piece of blotting paper with ammonium chloride before you cover it with another piece of metal. Hold the pile together with the rubber band. Screw the bulb into the socket. Connect the wire extending from one of the metals on the pile to one of the connections on the socket. Connect the wire extending from the other piece of metal on the pile to the second connection on the socket.

You will observe: The bulb in the socket lights up.

To keep the battery working, you must keep the blotting paper soaked with the ammonium chloride. This battery operates on the same principle as most batteries used in cars and homes although the materials used may vary. Electricity is conducted from one metal plate to another through a salt solution called an *electrolyte.* The metal plates are called *electrodes.* This type of battery is called a *voltaic* or *galvanic pile.*

HOW CAN YOU BRING A DEAD DRY CELL BACK TO LIFE?

Gather the following equipment: A dead dry cell; a flashlight bulb; a large jar about ¾ filled with warm water; a salt shaker filled with salt; a 6-inch length of bell wire; and a piece of cloth.

Follow this procedure: Dissolve all the salt in the jar of water. Punch several holes in the top of the dry cell and place it in the jar of water. Let it soak for an hour. Then take it from the water and dry it with the cloth.

Scrape the insulation back from both ends of the wire. Curl one end of the wire tightly around the grooves in the metal at the base of the bulb. Then, holding the glass portion of the bulb, place the metal bottom of the bulb against the positive terminal of the dry cell. Hold the other end of the wire against the bottom of the cell.

You will observe: The bulb lights up.

When a dry cell dies, it is usually because the electrolyte has dried out. You can revive it in the manner just described, but the cell is weaker. Its ability to cause a flow of electrons will not last long because the electrolyte will dry very quickly, due to the holes punched in the top of the cell.

HOW CAN YOU MAKE A LEAD STORAGE CELL?

Gather the following equipment: Two strips of lead, each 5 inches long and 1 inch wide; one 4-inch and two 10-inch strips of bell wire; a drinking glass a little over ¾ filled with water; two 1½-volt dry cells; a demonstration flashlight socket; a flashlight bulb; and 2 ounces of sulphuric acid.

WARNING: Sulphuric acid is extremely dangerous. It can burn your skin and put holes in your clothes and furniture. If any of the acid accidentally gets onto your skin, hold that area of your skin under running water for a minute or more.

Follow this procedure: Punch a small hole about ¼ of an inch from the top of each of the lead strips. Then bend that edge back on both lead strips so they will hold when hooked to the edge of the glass. Scrape the insulation back at the ends of all three lengths of wire. Attach one end of each of the 10-inch lengths of bell wire to the hole in each of the lead strips. Connect one end of the 4-inch length of bell wire to the positive terminal of one of the dry cells and the other end to the negative terminal of the other dry cell. Now connect the wire leading from one of the lead strips to the free terminal on one of the dry cells and connect the wire from the second lead strip to the free terminal on the other dry cell. Place the lead strips into the glass of water with the bent edges resting on opposite sides of the top edge of the glass. Pour the sulphuric acid into the glass. Wait 10 minutes. Then disconnect all the wires from the dry cells and connect the two coming from the lead strips to the connections on the demonstration socket. Screw the bulb into the socket.

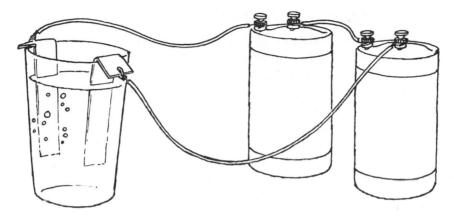

You will observe: The bulb lights up.

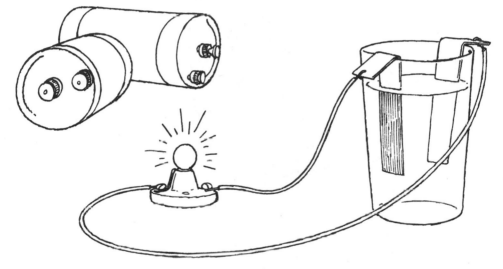

This type of cell, which is called a lead storage cell, is similar to the first cells ever used. Because the electrolyte spills easily and evaporates rapidly, scientists developed the dry cell which we now use so extensively. The lead storage battery, however, is still used in automobiles, where the running of the motor recharges the battery. You can recharge the cell you have just made by connecting it to the dry cells until one of the lead plates takes on a brownish color again.

A *cell* is one set of positive and negative plates. A *battery* consists of more than one cell. That is why, strictly speaking, it is more accurate to refer to a flashlight "battery" or any other single dry cell as a "cell."

HOW CAN YOU BUILD A FLASHLIGHT?

Gather the following equipment: A flashlight dry cell; a flashlight bulb; 5 inches of bell wire; and some cellophane tape.

Follow this procedure: Scrape the insulation from both ends of the wire. Make a coil of the wire at one end. Curl the other end of the wire tightly around the grooves at the base of the bulb. Tape the coiled end of the wire to the bottom of the dry cell. Then tape the remainder of the wire around the cell, except for a small portion just large enough to permit the grooves of the bulb to reach the positive terminal of the dry cell. Now press that portion of the wire, so that the bulb makes contact with the positive terminal of the cell.

You will observe: The bulb lights up.

HOW DO SWITCHES WORK?

Gather the following equipment: Two 1½-volt dry cells; a demonstration flashlight socket; a flashlight bulb; a knife switch (a kind of electric switch); three 10-inch lengths and one 3-inch length of bell wire.

Follow this procedure: Connect the equipment as shown in the illustration. Close the knife switch. Open it.

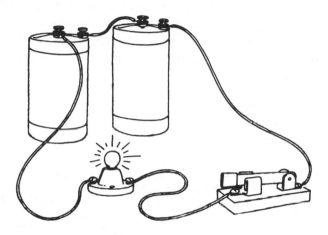

You will observe: When you close the knife switch, the light goes on. When you open it, the light goes off.

When you close the switch, you complete the circuit. There must be a closed circuit to have a current. All switches operate on the same principle.

HOW CAN YOU CONTROL A LIGHT WITH TWO SWITCHES?

Gather the following equipment: Two blocks of wood, each 3 inches square; two 3-inch strips and four 1-inch strips of metal (from the top and bottom of a can) ; 6 small screws; a demonstration flashlight socket; a flashlight bulb; a 1½-volt dry cell; and about 6 feet of thin, insulated copper wire, or more if you want the switches farther apart.

Follow this procedure: Assemble the equipment as shown in the illustration. Be sure to strip wires of insulation at all points where they are to be connected. Put both switches on the connections marked "X." Now try putting both switches on the connections marked "Z." Put one switch on "X" and the other on "Z."

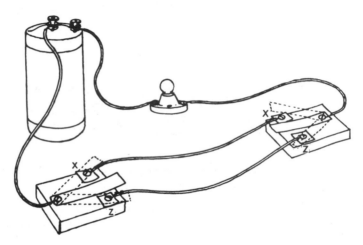

You will observe: When the switches are both on "X," the light is on. When the switches are both on "Z," the light is on. But when one switch is on "X" and the other on "Z," the light is off. In this manner you can turn the light on and off with either switch. It goes on when you complete the circuit and off when you break the circuit.

HOW CAN YOU WIRE IN SERIES?

Gather the following equipment: Two 1½-volt dry cells; two 10-inch lengths and three 4-inch lengths of bell wire; 3 demonstration flashlight sockets; and 3 flashlight bulbs.

Follow this procedure: Connect your equipment as shown in the illustration. Then loosen or remove one of the bulbs from its socket.

You will observe: When you have made all the connections and screwed all three bulbs tightly into the sockets, the circuit is closed and all three bulbs light up. If you loosen or remove one of the bulbs from its socket, the circuit will be open and all three bulbs will go out. By connecting the negative terminal of one cell to the positive terminal of another cell, you connect the source of voltage *in series.*

Series wiring is sometimes used for Christmas tree lights.

HOW CAN YOU WIRE IN PARALLEL?

Gather the following equipment: Two 1½-volt dry cells; 3 demonstration flashlight sockets; 3 flashlight bulbs; two 10-inch lengths and five 4-inch lengths of bell wire.

Follow this procedure: Connect your equipment as shown in the illustration. Then unscrew one bulb and observe what happens. Unscrew a second bulb.

You will observe: All three bulbs light up when the equipment is connected. When you unscrew any one bulb, the others remain lighted. When you unscrew two bulbs, the third remains lighted. As long as one bulb remains in its socket, there is a closed circuit and an electric current flows. In this experiment, you have connected the source of voltage in series and the circuit *in parallel.*

Parallel wiring is used in homes, offices and factories.

WHAT IS A SHORT CIRCUIT?

Gather the following equipment: Two 1½-volt dry cells; two 10-inch lengths and one 4-inch length of bell wire; a flashlight demonstration socket; and a flashlight bulb.

Follow this procedure: Scrape the insulation from the ends of all the lengths of wire and from an inch-long portion at the center of each of the 10-inch lengths. Place the two dry cells side by side and connect the negative terminal of the dry cell on the left to the positive terminal of the dry cell on the right with the 4-inch length of wire. Using one of the 10-inch lengths of wire, connect the positive terminal of the dry cell on the left with one of the connections on the socket. Use the other 10-inch length of wire to connect the second connection on the socket with the negative terminal of the dry cell on the right. Screw the bulb into the socket. Hold one of the wires at a point where the insulation is still on it and move it to the other wire so that the portions with bare copper on both wires touch each other.

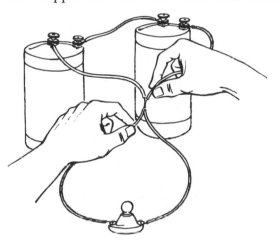

You will observe: The light goes out.

Electric current always takes the shortest route possible. The *short circuit* in this experiment cut the bulb out of the circuit. If you touched the bare wire at the point of shorting, you would discover that a short circuit produces a great amount of heat; in fact it can cause a fire. *Disconnect the wires from the dry cells as soon as you have finished the experiment.*

HOW CAN YOU MAKE AN INCANDESCENT BULB?

Gather the following equipment: A wide-mouthed jar; a cork, rubber cover, or piece of wood to fit the jar; 2 nails about 3 inches long or steel knitting needles; a 4-inch length of nichrome wire; three 1½-volt dry cells; two 4-inch and two 12-inch lengths of thin, insulated copper wire; and a hammer.

Follow this procedure: Place the three dry cells side by side. Connect the negative terminal of the dry cell on the left to the positive terminal of the dry cell in the middle with one of the 4-inch wires. Use the other 4-inch wire to connect the negative terminal of the dry cell in the middle with the positive terminal of the dry cell on the right. Hold the cover of the jar upside down and hammer the nails about 2 inches through the cover, about 1½ inches from each other. Fold the nichrome wire in half and twist the two halves around each other. Connect the twisted nichrome wire between the two nail heads. Turn the cover over so that the nail heads are now in the jar. Neither the nail heads nor the nichrome wire should touch the side or the bottom of the jar. Connect one of the 12-inch insulated wires from the point of the nail on the left to the positive terminal of the dry cell on the left. Connect the other 12-inch insulated wire to the other nail and to the negative terminal of the dry cell on the right.

You will observe: The nichrome wire filament glows.

The jar with the nichrome filament in it is actually a very simple type of incandescent bulb. Nichrome is a kind of steel which offers a high resistance to electrical current. When electrons have difficulty flowing through a conductor, their energy takes the form of heat and light. Thus, the nichrome gets red hot and glows when a current passes through it.

HOW CAN YOU BUILD AN ELECTRIC QUIZ GAME?

Gather the following equipment: Twenty-four paper clips; a shirt cardboard or any large sheet of cardboard or thin wood; about 18 feet of thin,
insulated electric wire; a 1½-volt dry cell; and a demonstration flashlight
socket with a flashlight bulb in it. You may need some cellophane tape, too.

Follow this procedure: Holding the cardboard lengthwise, attach 12
clips about an inch apart along the left side of it. Then attach 12 clips to
the right side of it, in a direct line with the corresponding clips on the left.
Number the clips down both sides from 1 to 12. Now cut the wire into
pieces long enough for you to make the following connections between the
clips on the left and those on the right:

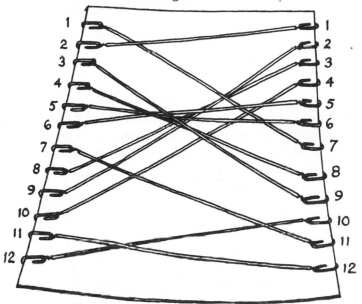

Scrape the insulation back from the ends of each length of wire as you
cut it. Make two tiny twists of wire around each clip so that the connection
is firm. When you have finished making all the connections, check to see
that there are no contacts between the bare copper of one wire and that of
another. If you find such a contact, place two or three strips of cellophane
tape between the two wires to serve as insulation.

Cut two 18-inch lengths of wire. Connect the end of one wire to the
positive terminal on the dry cell, and connect the end of the other to the
negative terminal. Connect the wire extending from the negative terminal
to one of the connections on the demonstration flashlight socket. Attach 12

inches of wire to the other connection on the flashlight socket. Turn the
cardboard over.

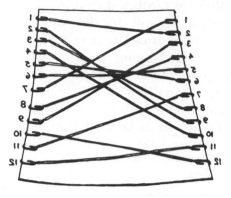

Devise a list of 12 questions. Write them on small slips of paper and
put them under each of the 12 clips on the left of the reverse side of the
cardboard. Write the answers to the questions on 12 more small slips of
paper. Put them under the appropriate clips on the right of the reverse side
of the cardboard — the answer to the first question under the second clip,
the answer to the second question under the ninth clip, and so on.

In one hand, hold the free end of the wire that is connected to the socket, and in the other hand, hold the free end of the wire that is connected to the positive terminal of the dry cell. Place the end of the wire in your left hand tightly against a clip over one of the questions. Then place the end of the wire in your right hand tightly against the clip on the correct answer.

You will observe: If you have placed the right-hand wire on the other end of the wire to which the question is attached, the bulb lights up.

To make the game more interesting, you can make up an unlimited number of sets of questions and answers. Instead of writing each question and each answer on separate pieces of paper, write them at the appropriate places on one sheet of paper an inch narrower and shorter than the sheet of cardboard. Then you can fit the whole question-and-answer sheet under the clips or remove it and replace it with another in a matter of seconds.

HOW CAN YOU BUILD A TELEGRAPH SET?

Gather the following equipment: A 1½-volt dry cell; 25 feet of thin, insulated wire; 2 iron bolts, each about 2 inches long; a nut to fit one of the bolts; four 1-inch nails; 3 small screws; 4 blocks of wood, each about 3 inches by 3 inches by ¼ of an inch; and 2 strips of metal, each about 2½ inches long and ½ inch wide (the metal may be cut from the top or bottom of a can).

Follow this procedure: Connect the equipment as indicated in the illustration. Be sure to scrape the insulation from the wires at all points of connection. Push the metal strip (or *key*, as this kind of switch is called in telegraphy) down on the screw. Release it.

You will observe: When you push the key down on the screw, you complete the circuit. This causes the electromagnet (the coil) to attract the metal strip (sounder) from the bolt on which it rests. As soon as the metal strip pulls away from the bolt below, the circuit is broken. The electromagnet then loses its power and the sounder falls back to the bolt. This completes the circuit again, with the result that the electromagnet again attracts the sounder. This happens many, many times each second, as long as you hold

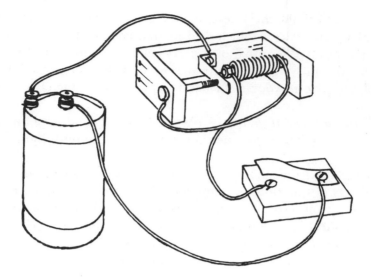

the key down against the screw; the sounder touches the magnet and the bolt in such quick succession that it makes a buzzing sound.

If you make a telegraph set with longer wires, you can keep the key in one room and the rest of the set, including the dry cell, in another room, and you can send a message from the first room to the second one.

To make communication possible with the telegraph, codes of dots and dashes have been developed. The most popular one is the International Morse Code, which is listed below:

A · —   N — ·
B — · · ·   O — — —
C — · — ·   P · — — ·
D — · ·   Q — — · —
E ·   R · — ·
F · · — ·   S · · ·
G — — ·   T —
H · · · ·   U · · —
I · ·   V · · · —
J · — — —   W · — —
K — · —   X — · · —
L · — · ·   Y — · — —
M — —   Z — — · ·

(There are slight variations in the American Morse Code.)

A dot is a very short sound that you make by pressing the key just long enough to get a sound and then releasing it immediately. A dash is a sound that lasts about three times as long as a dot; to make it, you hold the key down about three times as long as you would for a dot.

Telegraphers call the dots "dits" and the dashes "dahs." When they rattle off the letters very quickly, "A" sounds like "di-dah," "X" like "dah-di-di-dah," and so forth. Saying the code to yourself helps you memorize it. You can "talk" code this way with a friend who knows the code, too.

HOW CAN YOU BUILD A TELEGRAPH SET WITH A BULB?

Gather the following equipment: A 1½-volt dry cell; as much thin, insulated wire as you will need to place the set the way you want it; a strip of metal 3 inches long and ½ inch wide (from the top or bottom of a can) ; 2 small screws; a demonstration flashlight socket; a flashlight bulb; and a block of wood 3 inches square.

Follow this procedure: Assemble the equipment as in the illustration. Then press the bent metal switch down on the screw. Release it.

You will observe: When you press the switch, the circuit is completed and the light flashes on. When you release the switch, you break the circuit. The switch then springs up and away from the screw and the light goes off.

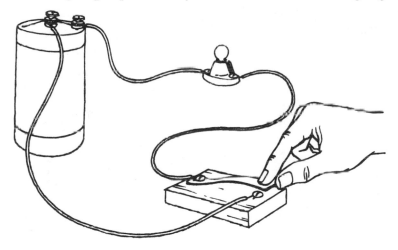

HOW CAN YOU WIRE A BELL FOR YOUR ROOM?

Gather the following equipment: A bell; a push button; about 25 feet of thin, insulated wire; a 1½-volt dry cell; a box of wood staples; and 4 small screws.

Follow this procedure: The length of the wires you should use in making connections depends on where you decide to place the button, the bell and the dry cell. The following lengths are suggestions. Place the dry cell on the floor inside your room, as near as possible to the corner where the door is hinged. Connect a 10-inch wire from the negative terminal on the dry cell to one of the connections on the push button. Connect a 7-inch wire to the other connection on the push button. Then screw the push button to the floor outside your room, as close as possible to the door hinges. Push the free wire from the push button through the space which appears between the door and the wall when the door is open. Then connect that wire to one of the connections on the inside of the bell. Connect a 10-inch wire from the second connection on the inside of the bell to the positive terminal of the dry cell. Now screw the bell to the inside of the door, near the bottom hinge. Staple those wires which are free and in the way to the floor or door, which-ever seems more convenient. Be sure to leave enough play for the door to open and close without pulling the connections loose. Step outside the door and put your foot on the push button.

You will observe: The bell on the inside of the door rings. The push button acts as the switch to complete the circuit.

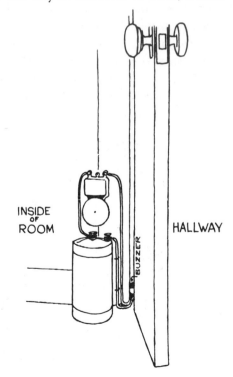

INSIDE OF ROOM

HALLWAY

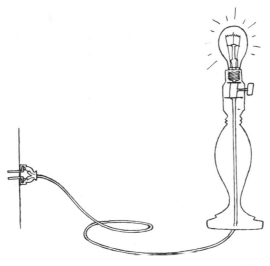

HOW CAN YOU WIRE A LAMP?

Gather the following equipment: A bulb socket; an incandescent bulb; enough house wire to lead from a nearby wall outlet to the place where you want to keep your lamp; a wall plug; a screw driver; a pocket knife; and a lamp stand.

WARNING: Never work on electric wires or connections while the wires are plugged into the wall outlet.

Follow this procedure: Pry the top half of the bulb socket from the bottom half, using the knife as a wedge if necessary. Push one end of the wire through the hole in the bottom half of the socket. Examine the end of the wire, and you will see that it is made up of two cords of copper, each covered by insulation. Separate the two cords to a distance of about ¾ of an inch from the end. Then strip the insulation from that ¾-inch portion of each cord. Pull the wire apart for another inch and tie a knot at the point where the cords begin to separate. Connect each of the stripped halves to one of the connecting screws on the top half of the socket. Make the connection by first loosening the screw, then turning the copper wire 1½ turns around it in a clockwise direction, and then tightening the screw. *Make sure that no bare copper from one cord is touching any bare metal to which the other cord is connected.* After you have made both connections, replace the bottom half of the socket, being sure to insert the insulating cardboard sleeve. Push (or pull) the other end of the wire through the lamp stand. Split and

49

strip the free end of the wire. Push it through the hole in the plug toward the prongs. When you have pushed it through far enough, knot the two wires at the point where they begin to separate. Twist each of the wires around one of the prongs. Twist it also 1½ turns in a clockwise direction around the screw behind the prong. Tighten the screws. Then screw the bulb into the lamp socket. Again, be sure that no patches of bare metal touch each other except at the connections. Put the plug into the wall outlet. Turn the switch on.

You will observe: The light goes on. The two wires are bound together, though separated by insulation, to make a complete circuit for the flow of electric current without the jumble which single wires would involve.

HOW CAN YOU COPPERPLATE A SAFETY PIN?

Gather the following equipment: A safety pin; 1 ounce of copper sulphate (available at a well-equipped drug store or a chemical supply house) ; 3 feet of thin, insulated wire; a drinking glass ¾ filled with warm water; glass stirrer; and two 1½-volt dry cells.

Follow this procedure: Clean the safety pin thoroughly with soap and water or alcohol. Dissolve the copper sulphate in the glass ¾ full of warm water. Be sure to wash it thoroughly immediately after using it. Place the

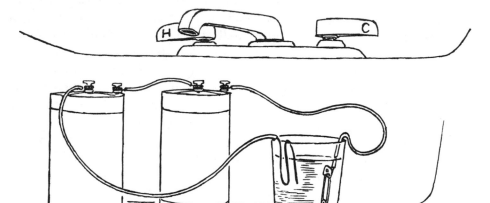

dry cells side by side behind the glass. Strip the insulation from the ends of a 4-inch long piece of wire, and use it to connect the negative terminal of the dry cell on the left with the positive terminal of the dry cell on the right. Attach one end of an 18-inch length of wire, after stripping the insulation, to the positive terminal of the dry cell on the left. Strip the insulation from about 6 inches of the other end of this wire. Fold this 6-inch portion on itself twice and place it in the glass, keeping it on one side. Connect one end of the remaining wire to the negative terminal of the dry cell on the right. Make a hook on the other end of the wire. Place the head of the safety pin on the hook and lower the pin into the glass so that it is completely submerged in the copper sulphate solution. Bend a small section of the wire above the pin so that it rests on the glass. Be sure that no part of the pin is in contact with the other copper wire. After 30 minutes or more, take the pin out of the solution with the wire hook, and wash it thoroughly.

You will observe: The safety pin is copperplated.

The copper sulphate solution serves as an electrolyte. Not only does it carry an electric current, but its molecules are actually broken down into their component parts by the current. This process is called *electrolysis.* The copper molecules are positively charged. The sulphur-and-oxygen molecules stay bound together in a chemical unit called a *radical.* The sulphur-and-oxygen radical has a negative charge. When a complete circuit is created, the copper molecules in the electrolyte, which are positive, are attracted to the safety pin, which is negative because of its connection to the negative terminal of one of the dry cells. Copper from the copper strip passes into the electrolyte, replacing the copper which settles on the safety pin.

HOW CAN YOU SILVERPLATE A KEY?

Gather the following equipment: A key; a piece of silver or a silverplated object which you no longer want; two 1½-volt dry cells; 3 ounces of silver nitrate (available in a well-equipped drug store or at a chemical supply house) ; a wide-mouthed quart jar; and about 3 feet of thin, insulated copper wire.

Follow this procedure: Fill the jar almost to the top with warm water. Dissolve the silver nitrate in the water. Place the two dry cells behind the jar. Connect the negative terminal of the dry cell on the left with the positive terminal of the dry cell on the right, using a 4-inch length of wire. Attach another length of wire from the positive terminal of the dry cell on the left to the piece of silver. Then place the silver in the jar, bending the wire above it so it will hook onto the glass. Connect another length of wire from the negative terminal of the dry cell on the right to the key. Place the key in the solution. Make a bend in the wire about 3 inches above the key so that the wire hooks onto the edge of the glass. Be sure that the silver and the key are not in contact with each other. After 30 minutes, remove the key from the solution.

You will observe: The key is silverplated.

The silver nitrate solution serves as an electrolyte which separates itself into silver molecules and nitrate radicals (nitrogen-and-oxygen molecules) . The silver molecules, having a positive electrical charge, are attracted to the key, which is negative because of its attachment to the negative terminal of one of the dry cells. Silver from the silverplated object passes into the electrolyte, replacing the silver that settles on the key.

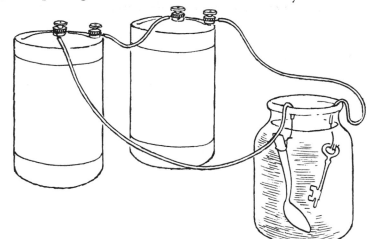

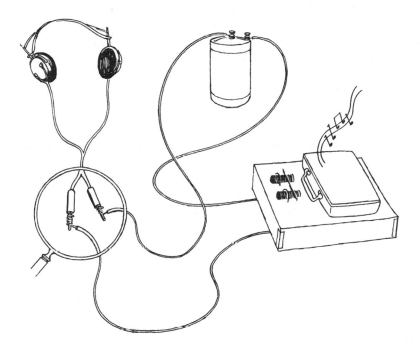

HOW CAN YOU BUILD A MICROPHONE?

Gather the following equipment: An empty cigar box, candy box or other similar box; 2 dead flashlight dry cells; a wooden pencil, preferably No. 2; a 1½-volt dry cell; 15 feet of thin, insulated wire; a pair of earphones or a receiver from an old-fashioned two-piece telephone; and a small radio, watch or table clock.

Follow this procedure: Cut the wire into two 3½-foot lengths and one 8-foot length. Whittle the wood from the pencil until you have an unbroken and uncovered 3-inch strip of pencil lead (graphite). Take the flashlight dry cells apart carefully until you uncover the carbon core of each of them. Turn the box upside down. Place the two pieces of carbon from the dry cells on top of it, parallel to each other and about 2 inches apart. Puncture holes in the box on both sides of each piece of carbon. From the underside of the box, thread one of the 3½-foot lengths of wire up through one of the holes, over a piece of carbon, and back down through the hole on the other side of the carbon; make sure to strip the insulation from the portion of the wire that is binding the carbon to the box. Tie the wire beneath the carbon in a loop under the box; this will serve the double purpose of keeping contact with the carbon and also holding it in place. Do the same thing with the other piece of carbon, using one end of the 8-foot length of wire. Draw the 3½-foot wire out from under the box and connect it to the negative terminal of the dry cell. Connect the second 3½-foot wire from the positive terminal of the dry cell to one of the wires on the earphones. You may have to unscrew a jack at the end of the wires on the headset. Examine the way the wires are attached to the jack and attach the wire leading from the dry cell to one of them. Connect the unattached end of the 8-foot wire to the other wire on the headset. Make sure that the two wires you have just connected to the headset are insulated against shorting at the places where the connections are close. Turn on the radio softly and place it, speaker down, on the box near the pieces of carbon. Place the pencil lead on the two pieces of carbon, perpendicular to them both. Put the earphones to your ears.

You will observe: You can hear sounds from the radio in your earphones.

The sounds from the radio cause the box to vibrate. The box, in turn, causes the two pieces of carbon to vibrate. The pieces of carbon cause the pencil lead to vibrate, opening and closing the complete circuit so rapidly that it causes the sounds the radio produces to be reproduced in the earphones with greater volume.

HOW CAN YOU MAKE A GENERATOR?

Gather the following equipment: A wire coat hanger; a new, unsharpened pencil; a large pencil sharpener; some cellophane tape; an empty thread spool; a coping saw; a small hammer; 4 carpet tacks; a demonstration flashlight socket; a flashlight bulb; 4 copper strips, 4 inches by ½ inch each; 2 small screws; 3 large, wide U-shaped magnets of the same size; about 30 feet of thin, insulated copper wire; 2 thin books of the same size; 2 thick books of the same size; and a square of wood, 10 inches or larger, on which to mount the above equipment. You may also need some toothpicks.

Follow this procedure: Saw the spool in half (1). Slide the two spools you now have onto the point end of the pencil and place them 1½ inches apart. Set the pencil aside.

From the hanger, form a rectangle such that the short sides are narrower than the space between the poles of the magnets. From the open short end, extend two 2-inch stubs spaced ¼ of an inch apart (2). Tape these extensions to the point end of the pencil (3).

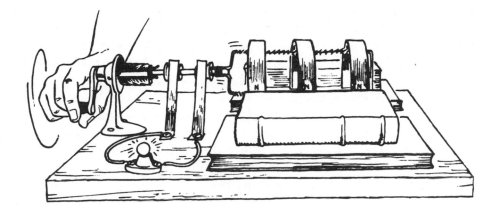

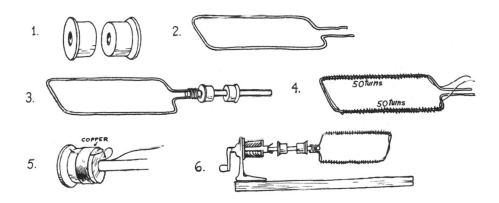

1.

2.

3.

4.   50 Turns
     50 turns

5.   COPPER

6.

Leaving 6 inches of wire free, wind 50 turns of wire along one long side of the hanger rectangle and then, without cutting the wire, wind 50 more turns on the other long rectangle side. The wire should now be back at the pencil end of the rectangle (4). Thread the wires (the two ends of the coil) through the hole in the first half spool. Scrape the insulation from the shorter of the two wires and secure it to the first spool by tightly tacking one of the copper strips over it (5). Clip the excess wire. Now thread the remaining wire through the second spool hole, scrape the insulation and secure it to the second spool with a second copper strip in the same manner as above. Clip the excess wire.

Mount the pencil sharpener on the wood with the handle extending over the edge. Wedge the eraser end of the pencil into the pencil sharpener with the toothpicks, making sure that the pencil turns with rotation of the handle (6). Attach the two remaining copper strips to the board so that they make sliding contact with the spools from the same side of the pencil. Attach a wire from each of these strips to a terminal on the flashlight socket. Place the 3 magnets with all the north poles on the same side in such a way that they form a tunnel over the rectangle with the coiled wire; make sure that neither the coat hanger wire nor the insulated wire touches the magnets. It is desirable for the rectangle, when turning, to be closer to the poles than to the center or top of the magnets. To achieve this, it may be necessary to place an edge of each thin book under all the north and south poles, respectively. Wedge the magnets in place by putting two thick books along the sides of the tunnel, horizontally, like book ends. Arrange the two copper strips so that each one now rests on one of the rings. Turn the handle of the sharpener rapidly.

You will observe: The light goes on and remains on as long as you turn the handle. When you stop turning the handle, the light goes out.

A *generator* is a machine designed to change mechanical energy into electrical energy. By turning the coils of wire between the poles of the magnets, you are intermittently starting and stopping their magnetic field and are thus inducing an alternating current into the wire. The circuit is completed by extending one of the wires (a.) from the coil to the metal on one of the rings, (b.) to the copper rubbing on that ring, (c.) to the wire leading to the bulb, (d.) through the bulb filament, (e.) through the wire leading to the other strip of metal, (f.) to the ring it is rubbing, (g.) to the wire connected to the ring, and (h.) back to the coils.

There are three rules governing the amount of electricity you can get with this kind of generator:

The greater the speed with which the magnetic field is broken, the greater is the amount of electricity produced.

The greater the number of coils in the wire, the greater is the amount of electricity produced.

The stronger the magnets, the greater is the amount of electricity produced.

HOW CAN YOU MAKE AN ELECTRIC MOTOR?

Gather the following equipment: Three 1½-volt dry cells; 2 large, wide U-shaped magnets of the same size; fourteen 1-inch nails; 2 thumbtacks; 2 paper clips; a new, unsharpened pencil; 2 small screws; some cellophane tape; a spool; 4 strips of thin copper (2 strips measuring 1 inch by 1½ inches, and 2 strips measuring 3 inches by ½ inch) ; 5 pieces of wood (1 piece measuring 3 inches by 10 inches; 2 pieces measuring 3 inches by 3½ inches, and 2 pieces measuring 2 inches by 3 inches) ; a 12-inch ruler; and 15 feet of thin, insulated copper wire.

Follow this procedure: Refer to the illustration below in assembling your equipment. Nail the wood together, as in the illustration. Tap a nail firmly into the center of each end of the pencil, being careful not to split the pencil. Open the paper clips, so that they each form the number "5." With the thumbtacks, mount the clips under each side of the top of the wooden frame you have made; mount them by the top of the "5," so that, together, they form a cradle for the nails at the ends of the pencil. The pencil should be able to roll freely. Being careful not to split the pencil, tap a nail firmly in the side of the pencil, 1 inch from the end of it. Tap another

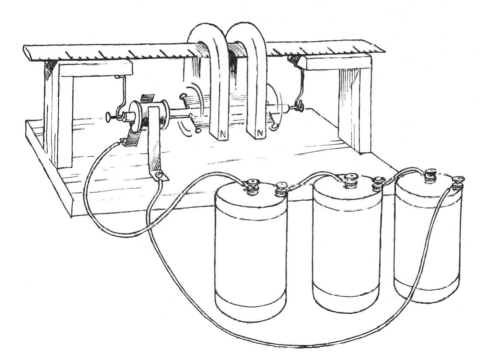

nail into the same side of the pencil, 2 inches away from the first nail and in line with it. Turn the pencil over and tap two nails into it directly opposite the nails on the other side. Place the dry cells in a row side by side. With a 4-inch wire, connect the negative terminal of the dry cell on the left to the positive terminal of the dry cell in the middle. Using another 4-inch wire, connect the negative terminal of the dry cell in the middle with the positive terminal of the dry cell on the right. Cut two 12-inch wires. Take the remaining wire, and holding 3 inches of it parallel to the pencil, wind 30 coils around the two nails on one side of the pencil. Without cutting the wire, wind 30 coils around the two nails on the other side, leaving 3 inches of wire parallel to the pencil, opposite the straight piece of wire on the other side of the pencil. Push the spool onto the long end of the pencil to within 1½ inches of the nails. Take the three inches of wire extending from the coils and mold it to the pencil, then up and over the nearer top and bottom edges, respectively. Cut and mold two strips of copper. Use each to cover and make contact with the end of one of the wires on the main body of the spool. The copper pieces should be ¼ of an inch away from each other on both sides of the main body of the spool. Tape the copper strips into place with lengthwise strips of tape. Leave at least ½ inch of the copper strips bare of tape and thus open to contact. Cradle the pencil on the clips. Screw one edge of each of the remaining two copper strips to the wood in such a way that when you lift them, they face each other, rest on, and rub against the copper strips on the spool. Connect a wire between the screw on one of the copper strips and the positive terminal of the dry cell on the left. Connect a wire between the screw on the other copper strip and the negative terminal of the dry cell on the right. Place the ruler so that it makes a bridge across the gap in the wood frame. Place the magnets one behind the other with the three north poles on the same side; lay them astride the ruler so that the coils of wire on the pencil are between the poles of the magnets.

You will observe: The pencil spins in its cradle.

An *electric motor* is a machine designed to change electrical energy to mechanical energy. The current goes from the dry cells, through the wire to the strip of copper (the *brush*), to the spool covered by copper (*commutator*), through the wire around the pencil (*armature*), back through the other side of the armature, through the commutator, through the other brush, and through the wire leading to the dry cells, thus making a complete circuit. The current running through the coils of the armature causes the armature to become an electromagnet with poles the same as those it faces on the field (U-shaped) magnets. Because the poles are the same, they repel each other. As soon as the north poles of the field magnets succeed in attracting the south pole of the electromagnet (which causes the pencil to turn), the current reverses itself. The south pole of the electromagnet then changes and becomes the north pole. A mutual repulsion is again set up between the field magnets and the electromagnet and the pencil turns again. The poles change so quickly that the pencil rotates continuously.

HOW CAN YOU MAKE A MODEL RAILROAD SIGNAL?

Gather the following equipment: A 1½-volt dry cell; an 8-inch length of wooden molding; a 6-inch length of thread; a piece of wood 3 inches long and 2 inches wide; a push button; a piece of cardboard 1½ inches long and ¼ of an inch wide; three 1-inch nails; one 1½-inch nail; 4 feet of thin, insulated copper wire; and a 4-inch by ¼-inch strip of metal cut from a can.

Follow this procedure: Assemble the equipment as in the illustration. Using your imagination, substitute other materials to make the signal itself more attractive. After you have assembled the material, push the button and then release it.

You will observe: When you push the button, the electromagnet attracts the metal strip, pulling the thread down and lifting the signal up. When you release the button, the electromagnet loses its magnetism, the thread rises and the signal drops.

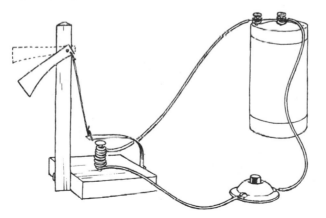

HOW CAN YOU MAKE A RHEOSTAT?
(A Device for Regulating an Electric Current)

Gather the following equipment: A 1½-volt dry cell; a pencil (preferably No. 2) ; a demonstration flashlight socket; a flashlight bulb; and 3 feet of thin, insulated copper wire.

Follow this procedure: Assemble the equipment as in the illustration. Move the unattached wire back and forth along the length of the exposed pencil lead.

You will observe: As you move the wire, the light gets brighter and dimmer. As you move toward the point of the pencil, that is, closer to one connection, the light gets brighter. As you move away from the point toward the other connection, the light gets dimmer.

The pencil lead in the rheostat you just made is the material that makes it possible to increase or dim the light. The pencil lead is a conductor of electricity but a poor one. The greater the distance the current flows in the pencil lead, the weaker it becomes. When you move the end of the wire away from the point of the pencil, you force the current to travel a greater distance through the pencil lead. This causes the current to grow weaker and the light to grow dimmer. Rheostats are often used to control the volume of sound in radios and television sets, and to make theatre lights grow dim slowly.

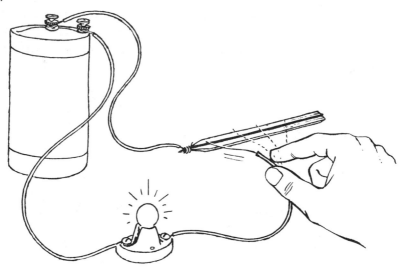

WHAT ARE THE KINDS OF ELECTRICITY WE USE?

There are two kinds of electric current — *direct current* (D.C.) and *alternating current* (A.C.).

Direct current has a steady flow in one direction. It was the first kind of electric current developed. It is not in extensive use today because it loses much of its energy when carried over great distances. It is still used, however, in automobile, flashlight, and other circuits which get their electricity from batteries or single cells, and for certain tasks, such as *electroplating* (like the copper- and silverplating which you have already done). The current must flow steadily in one direction for the metal in the electrolyte to be deposited on the object being electroplated.

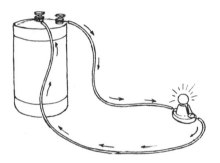

Alternating current reverses its flow in a circuit at regular intervals. Each two reversals (back and forth) is referred to as a *cycle*. The alternating

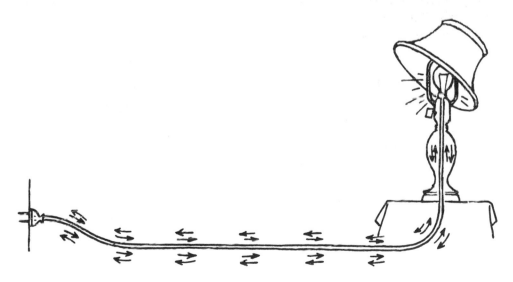

current most of us use in our homes has 60 cycles each second; this rate of alternation is fast enough so that we don't notice the flickering of our lights, as the current stops very very briefly between each cycle. We use alternating current more commonly because it can be carried over great distances without substantial loss. To do this, the current must be increased or decreased according to need by use of a device called a *transformer*.

WHAT IS A TRANSFORMER?

A transformer is a device used to build up or step down the current in an A.C. circuit. It consists of two coils of wire close to each other, one of which forms a complete circuit with a source of alternating current. The coil connected to the source of energy is called the *primary* coil, and the other coil, connected to the object utilizing the energy, is called the *secondary* coil. The alternating current flows from the source of energy through the primary coil and induces a current in the secondary coil. If there are more turns in the secondary coil than in the primary, the voltage is increased. Twice as many coils double the voltage, three times as many triple it, and so on. If there are fewer turns in the secondary coil than in the primary, the voltage is decreased in the same ratio. An *air-core* transformer has only air inside the primary and secondary coils. An *iron-core* transformer has iron inside the coils. The iron-core transformer increases and decreases voltage more efficiently than the air-core transformer.

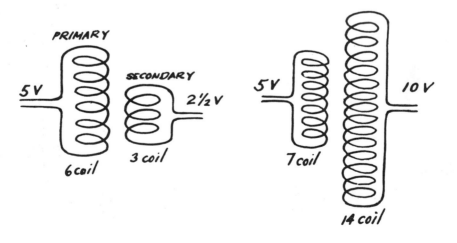

HOW CAN YOU READ A WATT-HOUR METER?

Electric current is measured in *amperes*. The pressure necessary to push it through a closed circuit is measured in *volts*. To determine the amount of electrical power being supplied, you multiply the amperage by the voltage. The result is measured in units called *watts*. The amount of electrical energy derived from one volt pushing one ampere for an hour is called a *watt-hour*. A watt-hour is a very small amount of energy. In one hour a reading lamp burns about 100 watts, a radio about 25, a refrigerator about 900. The average family uses many thousands of watt-hours each day. The company that supplies electricity to your home measures it, therefore, by a more convenient unit—the *kilowatt-hour,* which equals 1000 watt-hours.

Locate the watt-hour meter which measures the amount of electricity used in your home. It is usually in the basement or along one of the sides or back of your house, where the electric lines come in. It looks very much like the illustration below.

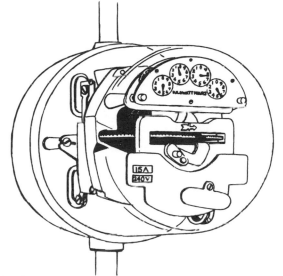

As electricity is used in your home, it causes a small motor to turn an aluminum disc in the meter. You can see the edge of the disc turning like a phonograph record just beneath the four dials. The more electricity being used, the faster the disc turns. The amount used is shown on the four dials. The dial on the far right shows the amount of kilowatt-hours up to 9. When that dial has gone around completely, it moves the hand on the dial just to the left to 1, and so on, until 99 kilowatt-hours have been used. Then the dial third from the right moves to 1. That dial shows how many kilowatt-hours have been used, up to 999. The dial on the left indicates the amount of kilowatt-hours used, up to 9999.

You read the meter by starting at the left and writing in order the last number passed by the hand on each dial. To determine how much electrical energy your home has used in one week, take two readings a week apart and subtract the first reading from the second.

ELECTRONICS

Electronics deals with the study of the movement of free electrons, especially through a vacuum, through gases, or through semiconductors — materials which conduct electricity better than insulators but not so well as conductors.

One of the earliest developments in what we now call electronics occurred in 1883, when Thomas Edison, who was then studying a weakness in the filament of his newly developed incandescent lamp, placed a strip of metal in the bulb and connected it to a battery. When the bulb was lighted, he found that electrons flowed from the filament to the metal strip, although there was no conductor between them. Edison did not continue to explore this phenomenon, which later became known as the "Edison effect." Shortly after the beginning of this century, however, other scientists did perform experiments to learn more about the Edison effect. Foremost among them were an Englishmen, Sir John Fleming, and an American, Dr. Lee De Forest.

Although great progress has been made in electronics since then, most experts agree that we have only begun to learn about it.

HOW CAN AN UNCONNECTED FLUORESCENT BULB GLOW?

Gather the following equipment: A fluorescent bulb and a piece of soft wool.

Follow this procedure: Take the fluorescent bulb into a dark room or closet and rub it vigorously with the wool.

WARNING: Be sure not to rub hard enough to break the glass; there is a chemical coating on the inside of it that can be very harmful.

You will observe: As you rub the bulb, it glows around the area where the wool touches it.

When you rub the glass, you pull some of the electrons away from the glass. This causes a positive charge on the glass. The imbalance pulls electrons from inside the tube toward the glass.

A fluorescent bulb is a long glass tube with a phosphor coating on the inside of the glass. The ends of the tube are *electrodes* (metal plates) ; a current of electrons flows between them when the tube is part of a closed circuit. The tube itself is filled with mercury vapor. As the electrons "shoot" through the tube, they bump into the atoms of mercury vapor, which then emit *ultraviolet rays* (a type of invisible light ray) . These, in turn, cause the phosphor coating to glow.

HOW DOES AN ELECTRON TUBE WORK?

WARNING: *This experiment should be performed ONLY UNDER THE DIRECT SUPERVISION OF A COMPETENT ADULT.*

Gather the following equipment: A burned-out electron tube (radio tube) ; a small hammer; a glass cutter; and a small paper bag. Use a hack saw instead of the glass cutter if the tube has a metal bulb.

Follow this procedure: Use the glass cutter to scrape a line around the glass where the bulb meets the base of the tube. Then, holding the base, place the bulb in the bag and tap it gently with the hammer until all the glass has been removed. Be careful not to destroy the insides of the bulb in the process. Examine the parts of the tube.

You will observe: When the glass breaks, you hear a "pop." On examination, you see that the parts that were enclosed by the bulb form two or more circuits extending from the prongs at the base of the tube.

In the simplest type of electron tube, the filament in the center is the negative electrode (*cathode*) . When a current flows through and heats the cathode, it emits electrons. The plate closest to the outside is the positive electrode (*anode*) ; it attracts the flow of electrons from the cathode. Sometimes there are wire meshes, called *grids,* between the anode and cathode; their purpose is to help regulate the number of electrons that reach the anode.

To prevent the cathode from burning up by combining with the oxygen in the air when the cathode is heated, most of the air is removed from the tube just before it is sealed. That is why the electron tube is sometimes called a *vacuum tube.* The "pop" you hear when the tube breaks is the air rushing in.

An electron tube which has only an anode and a cathode is called a *diode.* A tube which has an anode, a cathode and one grid is called a *triode.* A tube with an anode, cathode and two grids is a *tetrode,* and one with an anode, cathode and three grids is a *pentode.* There are also electron tubes with a number of other combinations of electrodes and grids, such as tubes with two anodes and two cathodes, called *duodiodes.* Electron tubes are designed according to special needs in performing a variety of functions. Among the various kinds of electron tubes are *oscillators,* which generate *radio waves* (very long invisible light waves) ; *modulators,* which blend audible waves with radio waves; *amplifiers,* which step up current to increase volume of sound; and *detectors,* which select audible waves from radio waves serving as carrier waves.

WHAT ARE SOME ELECTRONIC SYMBOLS?

Diagrams of electronic apparatus are called *schematics*. Because schematics would be extremely difficult, if not impossible, to read without some kind of a code, symbols have been devised for every type of electronic apparatus. The following is a chart of some of the symbols a beginner is likely to come across.

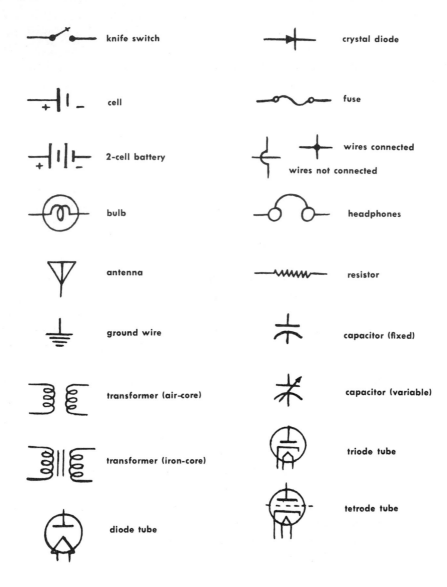

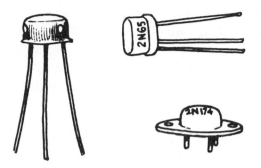

WHAT ARE TRANSISTORS?

The reason that certain materials are good conductors is that the electrons in the outermost orbit of their atoms, that is, the ones farthest from the nucleus, are held loosely. These electrons, therefore, can move freely. When a voltage is applied, many of them flow in a particular direction, thus constituting an electrical current. By contrast, the electrons in the atoms of materials which are insulators are held tightly. Even under the pressure of voltage, very few of them can be made to move freely.

In the atoms of semiconductors, such as selenium, germanium and silicon, the electrons are held less tightly than in insulators, but not so loosely as in conductors. Under certain conditions, these electrons free themselves and move in small quantities as negative charges. Once an atom or group of atoms bound together loses or gains one or more electrons, it becomes an *ion*. If it loses electrons, it is a *positive* ion; if it gains electrons, it is a *negative* ion. The ions in semiconductors also move.

Scientists can increase the unidirectional (one-way) movement of the electrons or the ions in semiconductors, thus making them better conductors and more valuable as electronic components. They do this by adding a tiny amount of some other substance to each *crystal* of the semiconductor. (Crystals are regular, smooth-faceted structural units of many solids; they are composed of groups of molecules.) When the substance that is added, because of the structure of its atoms, adds usable electrons to the crystal, it becomes an *n-type* crystal. When the substance added is lacking in electrons, and therefore adds positive ions, it is a *p-type crystal*. Arsenic is often added to make n-type crystals and gallium to make p-type crystals. These crystals can be used independently of each other or together in electronic circuits.

When they are combined in crystal "sandwiches," two of one and one of the other (npn or pnp), they are called *transistors*.

Transistors can perform the same functions in electronic circuits as electron, or vacuum tubes. Among the advantages of transistors are that they cause less heat than vacuum tubes, they last much longer than vacuum tubes, and most important, they are smaller than vacuum tubes. They permit the construction of smaller, more compact electronic apparatus, such as transistor radios and electronic brains.

WHAT ARE RESISTORS?

Most components in an electronic circuit, including the wires, offer some resistance to the flow of current; each component decreases the flow in proportion to the amount of resistance it offers. This is often an unavoidable disadvantage. Sometimes, however, parts of an electronic circuit require additional resistance to prevent their being damaged by a large amount of current. This resistance is supplied by a *resistor,* or high-resistance conductor, such as nichrome.

Resistance is measured in units called *ohms;* the symbol for ohms is Ω, the letter *omega* in the Greek alphabet. Sometimes the measurement *megohm* (one million ohms) is used. A color code in the form of stripes at one end of the resistor indicates the number of ohms of resistance offered by the resistor.

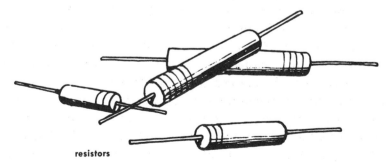

resistors

WHAT ARE CAPACITORS?

A *capacitor,* sometimes known as a *condenser,* is an electronic component that stores up electrical charges. It consists basically of two plates which are conductors, separated by an insulator. The insulator, which is called the *dielectric,* is usually air, mica, paper or oil. Capacitors store electrical charges in the dielectric. *Capacitance,* the amount of charge stored in the dielectric, is measured in *farads;* the symbol for farads is f. Most requirements for capacitance in electronic circuits, however, are for millionths of a farad, or for millionths of millionths of a farad. A *microfarad,* represented in symbol as mf, equals one millionth of a farad; a *micromicrofarad,* represented in symbol as mmf, equals one millionth of a millionth of a farad.

A *variable* capacitor is one which can change its capacitance as needed in the circuit at different times. One of the most common functions of variable condensers is the tuning of radio receivers to a desired frequency. A *fixed* condenser always maintains the same capacitance.

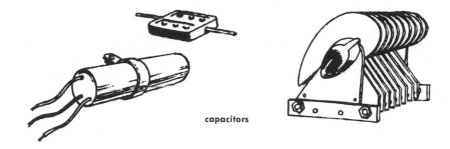

capacitors

WHAT ARE RADIO WAVES?

Radio waves are a type of *electromagnetic radiation* — a form of energy given off in waves by subatomic particles (see page 76). Waves of electromagnetic radiation are called *transverse;* this means that they vibrate perpendicular to the direction in which they are traveling. The length of the wave, that is, the distance between the crest of one wave and that of the next, varies enormously within the entire range of electromagnetic radiation, which is called the *electromagnetic spectrum.* All electromagnetic waves, regardless of their length, travel at the same speed: 186,000 miles per second. Since this is so, the *frequency*, that is, the number of waves per second, depends on the length: the shorter the wave, the higher the frequency and vice versa.

In roughly the central portion of the electromagnetic spectrum are waves of lengths which can be seen by the human eye; these are light waves. At either end of the spectrum are waves of lengths which are too short or too long to be seen by the human eye. Those which are too short to be seen include ultraviolet rays, X rays, beta rays, gamma rays, and cosmic rays. These rays have the power of penetrating solid materials, and they are harmful to living creatures. The waves which are too long to be seen include infrared rays and radio waves. Radio waves range in length from less than $\frac{1}{8}$ of a mile to more than $2\frac{1}{2}$ miles. Radio waves do not penetrate solid materials. There has been evidence recently, however, that they can be harmful when beamed at certain organs in the body, such as the brain.

The amount of electromagnetic radiation given off by subatomic particles varies according to the energy level of these particles. The higher the energy level, the more electromagnetic radiation is given off. The sun and stars are sources of stupendous amounts of electromagnetic radiation. All the light and heat on earth are traceable ultimately to the electromagnetic radiation of the sun. The subatomic particles of materials conducting an electric current are at an energy level high enough to give off considerable amounts of electromagnetic radiation. Thus, electromagnetic waves, including radio waves, can be generated by means of electricity. Radio waves, partially because of their length, travel through the air over great distances, and are very useful, therefore, as carrier waves in radio broadcasting. Radio stations are assigned specific frequencies which they may use.

HOW ARE RADIO WAVES USED FOR BROADCASTING?

The basic principle of radio broadcasting is that sounds are converted into electrical impulses at the broadcasting station, are sent out and carried through the air on radio waves, and are picked up and reconverted into sounds by the radio receiver.

Sound consists of vibrations caused by friction. The human voice, for example, consists of sounds caused by friction between air exhaled from the lungs and the vocal cords. These vibrations set up disturbances in air, which are sound waves. Sound waves are not electromagnetic; they are mechanical. Unlike electromagnetic waves, they are not transverse, but *longitudinal*, that is, they vibrate in the same direction in which they are traveling. Sound waves travel at a speed of about 1,100 feet per second, and they vary in length and frequency. Sound waves of frequencies that cannot be heard by the human ear are called *ultrasonic*.

At the broadcasting station, sounds are amplified by the microphone and are then combined with carrier waves. The sound waves cause slight irregularities in the carrier waves — a process called *modulation*. When the irregularities caused by the sound waves affect the frequency of the carrier waves, the broadcast is of the FM or *frequency modulation* type. When they affect the *amplitude* (the distance between the crest and base of a wave) of the carrier waves, the broadcast is of the AM or *amplitude modulation* type. The modulated carrier waves are then sent out by the transmitter.

The antenna of the receiver picks up the modulated carrier waves and conducts them inside the radio receiver. In the loud-speaker, they pass through an electromagnet; as they pass through, they set up vibrations which disturb the air, causing sound waves identical to those which entered the microphone at the broadcasting station. This is a vastly oversimplified explanation of the process of broadcasting; the actual mechanisms involved and the numerous phases in transmission and reception are of a complexity beyond the scope of this book.

HOW CAN YOU MAKE A SIMPLE RADIO?

Gather the following equipment: About 100 feet of thin, insulated copper wire, a 350-micromicrofarad variable capacitor (available at radio repair shops), a pair of electromagnetic-type headphones or a discarded telephone receiver, a germanium crystal of the kind designated 1N34, an empty cardboard tube from a roll of toilet tissue, and a piece of wood large enough to mount the above equipment.

Follow this procedure: Assemble the equipment as indicated in the schematic below. Then put on the headphones and slowly turn the knob on the capacitor.

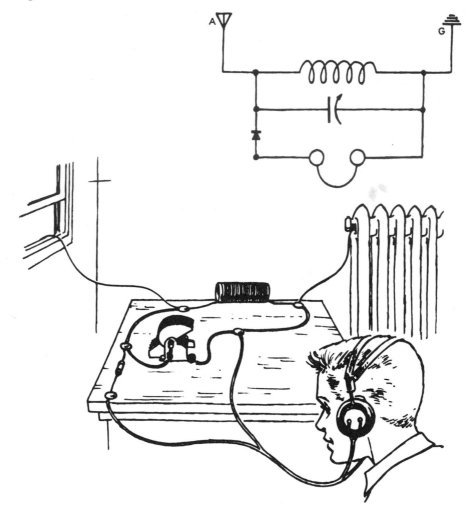

You will observe: You pick up several radio stations.

The antenna and coil pick up the radio waves. The capacitor adjusts the frequency of radio waves picked up by the antenna and coil. In this manner, you select different radio stations. The crystal serves as a detector; it allows those frequencies on the radio waves that can be changed into audible sound waves to come through to the headphones as stronger and weaker electrical impulses. The mechanism inside the headphones serves to change the electrical impulses to mechanical energy, causing sound waves, which you hear as voices, music or other sounds.

NUCLEAR ENERGY

Nuclear energy is energy that is released when atoms of one element are changed into atoms of other elements.

An atom is the tiniest bit of an element which has all the properties of that element. Atoms are so tiny that many billions of them are needed to make up a piece of matter the size of a pinhead. As tiny as they are, however, they are composed of even tinier parts—*protons, neutrons, electrons,* and others.

Protons are positively charged particles, held in a bundle together with the neutrons, which are uncharged particles. This bundle is called the nucleus. Electrons are negatively charged particles which circulate around the nucleus. Normally, an atom contains the same number of protons and electrons. Thus the positive and negative charges balance each other so that the practical effect is the same as if the atom had no charge at all. When an atom gains or loses one or more electrons, however, the charges of the protons and electrons no longer counterbalance each other; such an atom is known as an *ion* and has a charge.

The kind of element, of which any given atom forms a part, depends on the number of protons in the nucleus of the atom. When this number changes, the atom becomes an atom of another element. The nuclei of atoms of the same element sometimes vary in the number of neutrons they contain. Atoms that vary like this are called *isotopes*. Most hydrogen atoms, for example, have one proton and no neutrons in their nuclei, but occasionally hydrogen atoms are found with a neutron as well as a proton in the nucleus. This second type of hydrogen is called *deuterium*.

Atoms of some elements change themselves by shooting out rays and particles. This is called *decaying* or, more popularly, *radioactivity*. Radioactive elements are called *unstable*. The radioactive element you are likely to come across most commonly is radium. It is often used in paint on the numbers and hands of watches. Its radiation causes a glow which can be seen in the dark.

Scientists have found two other ways of changing atoms to get energy.

One is called *fission*. Fission is the splitting of atoms and can occur naturally as the result of radioactivity. Scientists can achieve fission in an *atomic reactor,* sometimes called an *atomic pile.* The U-235 isotope of uranium is one of the elements most commonly used for fission. Fission occurs when pieces of a suitable element are brought together to create what is called a *critical mass.* When this happens, a neutron escaping from one atom strikes the nucleus of another atom with such force that it splits the nucleus into two halves which, with the electrons, form new lighter-weight elements. This process also releases energy and one, two or more neutrons, which bombard other atoms, causing them to split, release more energy and more neutrons, and so on. This is called a *chain reaction.* When it is controlled, it is a source of tremendous amounts of usable energy. When it is uncontrolled, the energy is released so rapidly that it causes an explosion. The atom bomb uses the process of fission. "Nuclear energy" is a more accurate term than "atomic energy," because it is the nucleus that yields the most energy.

If a stable element is placed in an atomic pile while a chain reaction is occurring, its atoms do not split; scientists have found, however, that the bombarding neutrons frequently adhere to the nuclei of the stable element. The result sometimes is the creation of radioactive isotopes *(radioisotopes) ,* which have many uses in medicine and agricultural research. The radioisotopes are often used in these fields as *tracers.* By placing them inside a plant or human body and watching their progress with special instruments, research workers and doctors can observe the functioning of the organ into which they are placed. The atoms of each different radioisotope decay at a definite rate. Thus the amount of a particular radioisotope found in an object, such as an archeological find, can be used as a basis for calculating the age of the object. Carbon 14 is the radioisotope commonly used for this purpose.

The second method of changing atoms to get energy is called *fusion.* Fusion is the welding together of small atoms under tremendous pressure and heat, on the order of 50 million degrees C. Nuclear energy is needed to attain such heat. The small atoms combine to form fewer but larger atoms of another element. The deuterium isotope of hydrogen is used for fusion, and the element formed is helium. The hydrogen bomb uses the process of fusion, which yields more energy than any other process; fusion is the source of energy of the sun and stars. Scientists are trying to learn how to control fusion so that it can be used for nonexplosive purposes.

HOW CAN YOU BUILD A GEIGER COUNTER?

Gather the following equipment: A 300-volt Geiger tube (available at scientific supply houses) ; three 300-volt batteries; a .001 microfarad oil-filled capacitor; a pair of crystal headphones; a switch; a 1-megohm resistor; about 4 feet of insulated copper wire; some solder; a soldering iron; some rubber tape; a radium-painted watch; and a wooden board large enough to mount all the above equipment.

Follow this procedure: Assemble the equipment as indicated in the schematic below. Be sure to keep the switch in the "off" (open) position until you have made all the connections. Be sure also to cover all exposed wires with the rubber tape once you have made the connections.

GEIGER TUBE

WARNING: Place only one hand at a time on the apparatus after you have made the connections to the batteries to prevent shorting of the circuit through your body and consequently a serious shock.

Close the switch and place the tube near the watch.
You will observe: You hear a clicking in the headphones.

A Geiger tube has two electrodes in a gas-filled bulb. When it is placed near a radioactive substance, such as radium, shooting particles radiate through the gas, ionizing the atoms of the gas as they pass through. The ions have a charge, which causes a flow of current between the electrodes. The mechanism inside the headphones converts the flow of current into audible clicks. Each click is referred to as one *count* and corresponds to one burst of ionizing radiation.

The Geiger counter is named for one of its inventors, the German scientist Hans Geiger.

HOW CAN YOU TEST FOR RADIOACTIVE FALLOUT IN YOUR NEIGHBORHOOD?

Gather the following equipment: The Geiger counter you made or a professional instrument (which might be available at school or at your local Civil Defense center) ; a clean can; some very wide cellophane tape; and a cookie sheet.

Follow this procedure: Wind the cellophane tape around the cookie sheet with the gummed side up until you have covered the entire top surface of the sheet. Test the surface with the Geiger counter to determine the

amount of radioactivity on it. To do this, hold the counter close to the cookie sheet for one minute. Write down the count. Place the cookie sheet, gummed side up, outside your house—in the back yard, on the roof, or anywhere else where it won't be disturbed. Wait a full day. Then cut the tape from the top of the tin. Place it in the can and burn it. Test the residue with the Geiger counter. Subtract any count you may have gotten the previous day from this second count.

You will observe: The count you get after the subtraction represents the amount of radioactive fallout during the day the cookie sheet was outside. The burning of the cellophane tape served merely to concentrate the radioactivity, which cannot be burned away.

There is always some radioactivity in the air. A large percentage of it comes from natural causes, and is called natural background radiation. Some of it is also man-made, however, and comes chiefly from test explosions of atomic and hydrogen bombs. Most scientists are concerned about the rising level of radioactive fallout as a result of these test explosions. While they all agree that too much radioactive fallout can be dangerous to the population of the world, there is little agreement among them on how much is "too much" and even on how properly to calculate the present amounts.

TABLE OF ELEMENTS

Name of Element	Symbol	Atomic Number (number of protons)
Actinium	Ac	89
Aluminum	Al	13
Antimony	Sb	51
Americium*	Am	95
Argon	A	18
Arsenic	As	33
Astatine	At	85
Barium	Ba	56
Berkelium*	Bk	97
Beryllium	Be	4
Bismuth	Bi	83
Boron	B	5
Bromine	Br	35
Cadmium	Cd	48
Calcium	Ca	20
Californium*	Cf	98
Carbon	C	6
Cerium	Ce	58
Cesium	Cs	55
Chlorine	Cl	17
Chromium	Cr	24
Cobalt	Co	27
Copper	Cu	29
Curium*	Cm	96
Dysprosium	Dy	66
Einsteinium*	E	99
Erbium	Er	68
Europium	Eu	63
Fermium*	Fm	100
Fluorine	F	9
Francium	Fr	87
Gadolinium	Gd	64
Gallium	Ga	31
Germanium	Ge	32
Gold	Au	79
Hafnium	Hf	72
Helium	He	2

* Man-made elements.

TABLE OF ELEMENTS (Continued)

Name of Element	Symbol	Atomic Number (number of protons)
Holmium	Ho	67
Hydrogen	H	1
Indium	In	49
Iodine	I	53
Iridium	Ir	77
Iron	Fe	26
Krypton	Kr	36
Lanthanum	La	57
Lawrencium*	Lw	103
Lead	Pb	82
Lithium	Li	3
Lutetium	Lu	71
Magnesium	Mg	12
Manganese	Mn	25
Mendelevium*	Md	101
Mercury	Hg	80
Molybdenum	Mo	42
Neodymium	Nd	60
Neon	Ne	10
Neptunium*	Np	93
Nickel	Ni	28
Niobium	Nb	41
Nitrogen	N	7
Nobelium*	No	102
Osmium	Os	76
Oxygen	O	8
Palladium	Pd	46
Phosphorus	P	15
Platinum	Pt	78
Plutonium*	Pu	94
Polonium	Po	84
Potassium	K	19
Praseodymium	Pr	59
Promethium	Pm	61
Protoactinium	Pa	91
Radium	Ra	88
Radon	Rn	86

TABLE OF ELEMENTS (Continued)

Name of Element	Symbol	Atomic Number (number of protons)
Rhenium	Re	75
Rhodium	Rh	45
Rubidium	Rb	37
Ruthenium	Ru	44
Samarium	Sm	62
Scandium	Sc	21
Selenium	Se	34
Silicon	Si	14
Silver	Ag	47
Sodium	Na	11
Strontium	Sr	38
Sulphur	S	16
Tantalum	Ta	73
Technetium	Tc	43
Tellurium	Te	52
Terbium	Tb	65
Thallium	Tl	81
Thorium	Th	90
Thulium	Tm	69
Tin	Sn	50
Titanium	Ti	22
Tungsten	W	74
Uranium	U	92
Vanadium	V	23
Xenon	Xe	54
Ytterbium	Yb	70
Yttrium	Y	39
Zinc	Zn	30
Zirconium	Zr	40

INDEX

electromagnet, 17-18
  permanent magnet, 19-20
electromagnetic waves, 71-72
electron, 24, 76
electronics, 65-75
electronic symbols, 68
electron tube, 67
electrophorus, 31
electroplating, 61
  copperplating, 50-51
  silverplating, 52
electroscope, 29-30
elements, 7
  table of, 81-83
  unstable, 76

farad, 71
field magnets, 59
field of force, magnetic, 12
filament, 42, 67
fission, 77
fixed capacitor, 71
flashlight, 36
fluorescent bulb, 66
frequency modulation, 73
fuse, 41
fusion, 77

galvanic pile. *See* voltaic pile.
gamma rays, 72
Geiger counter, 83-84, 78, 79-80
generator, 54-56
geographic poles, 21-22
grid, 67

hydrogen bomb, 77

incandescent bulb, 42
infrared rays, 72
insulator, 28, 69
ions, 69
iron-core transformer, 62
isotopes, 76-77

kilowatt, 63

kilowatt-hour, 63

lead storage cell, 34-35
light waves, 72
lines of force, magnetic, 12
loadstone, 6
longitudinal waves, 73

magnetic field, 12
magnetic lines of force, 12
magnetic poles, 13-15
magnetism, 6-25
  attraction of, 7
  explanatory theories about, 24
  feeling the force of, 11
  induction of by electricity,
                    17-18, 19-20
  invisibility of, 12
  materials affected by, 7
  penetration of materials by, 8-10
  seeing the effects of, 12
magnetite, 6
magnets
  cutting of, 23
  electromagnets, 17-18
  field, 59
  permanent, 19-20, 24
  poles of, 13-15
  temporary, 15-16, 24
megohm, 70
microfarad, 71
micromicrofarad, 71
microphone, 53-54
model railroad signal, 59
modulation, 73
modulator, 67
molecule, 24
Morse code, 46

neutrons, 76-77
n-type crystal, 69-70
north pole, 13, 21-22
nuclear energy, 76-80
nucleus of atom, 24, 76